Thank you for purchasing the Word Bank, a tool to help build your vocabulary. This workbook is intended for all language learners. It was crafted as an aid to help learners track and review vocabulary.

Learning a new language can be fun, but it also requires some effort to learn large amounts of common vocabulary. By the end of this workbook, you will have reached a significant milestone. Having learned 4000 words, you can carry on various conversations in your target language. Continued practice and use of the language will help you grow in fluency.

TIPS FOR USE:

Add new words to the word bank as you learn them. You can include notes, definitions or tips on pronunciation. Review your word bank entries and find ways to use your new vocabulary daily.

Use this workbook to set and track your language goals. Setting goals can help you stay motivated while learning.

A good way to learn new words is by watching television or reading books in the target language. Choose a learning style that works for you.

Practice Practice Practice. Fluency improves drastically with daily use. Find a speaking partner and practice using your target language daily. Practice when you're alone by talking or thinking in the target language. You can talk aloud about what you will do today or a topic you have been studying. A helpful way to practice when you are alone is to record yourself speaking and review.

However you choose to learn new words, use this workbook to build your vocabulary.

My Learning Journey

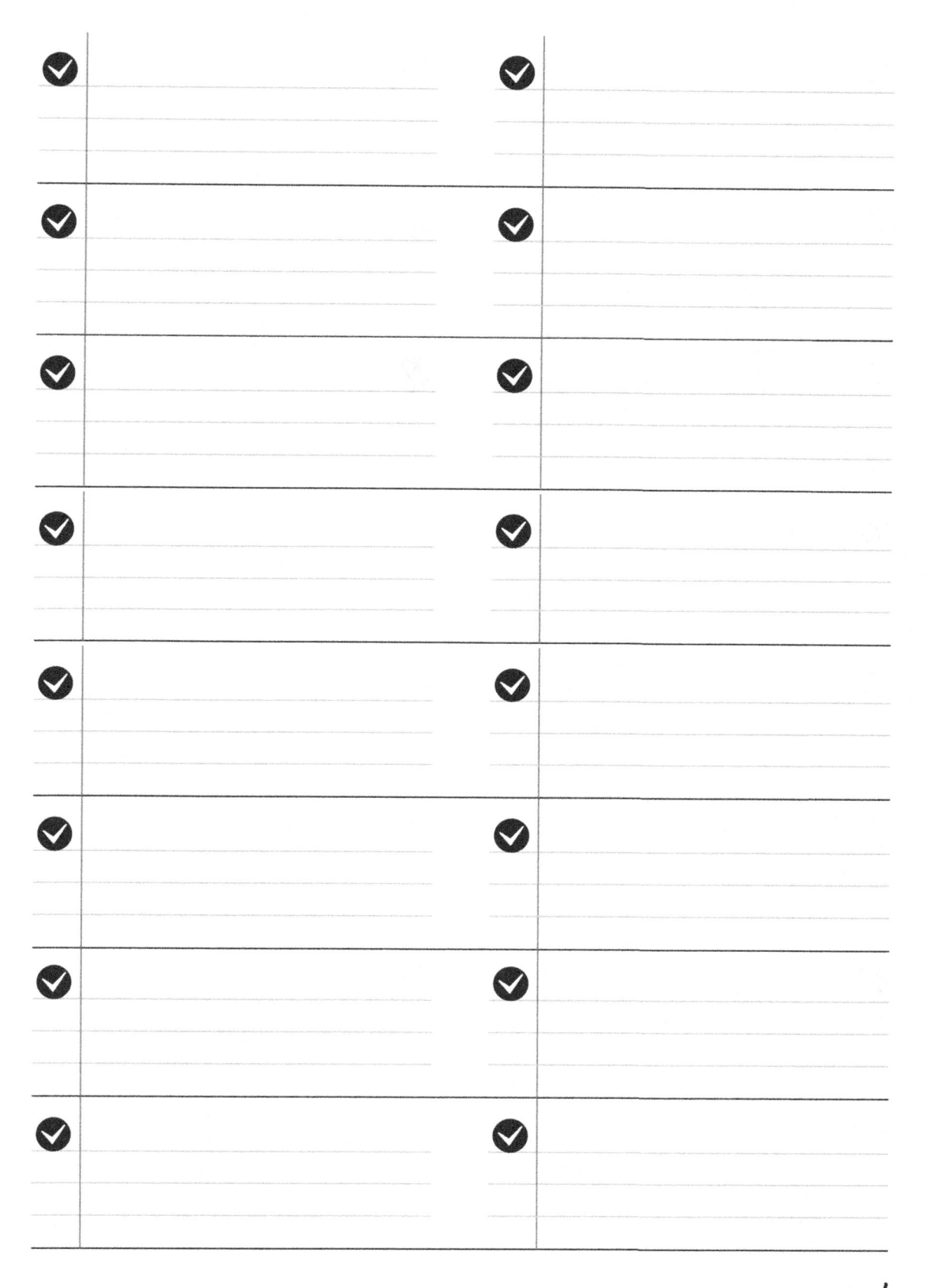

Congradulations!
16 words learned

My Learning Journey

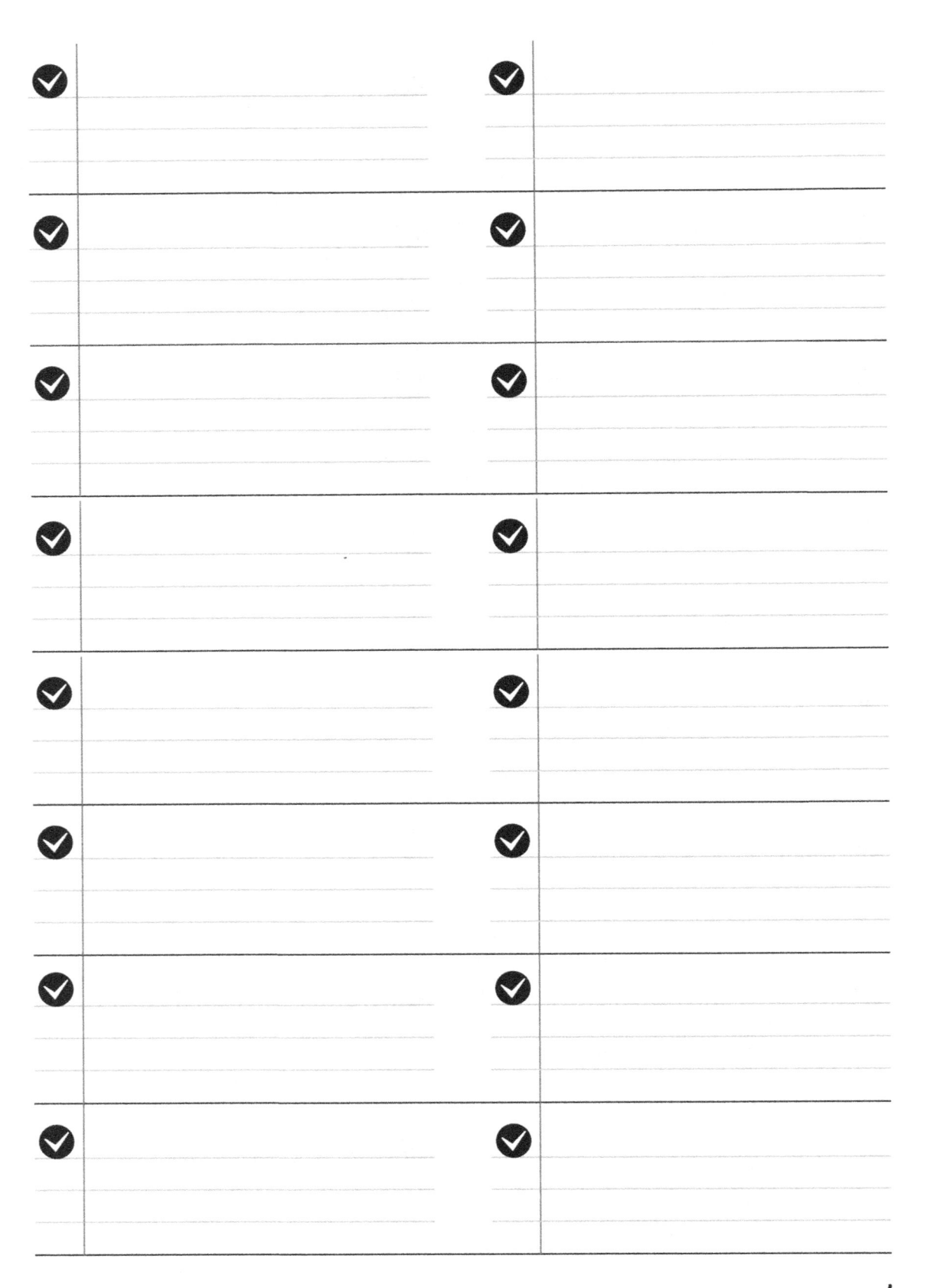

Congradulations!
32 words learned

My Learning Journey

Congradulations!
48 words learned

My Learning Journey

Congradulations!
64 words learned

My Learning Journey

Congradulations!
80 words learned

My Learning Journey

Congradulations!
96 words learned

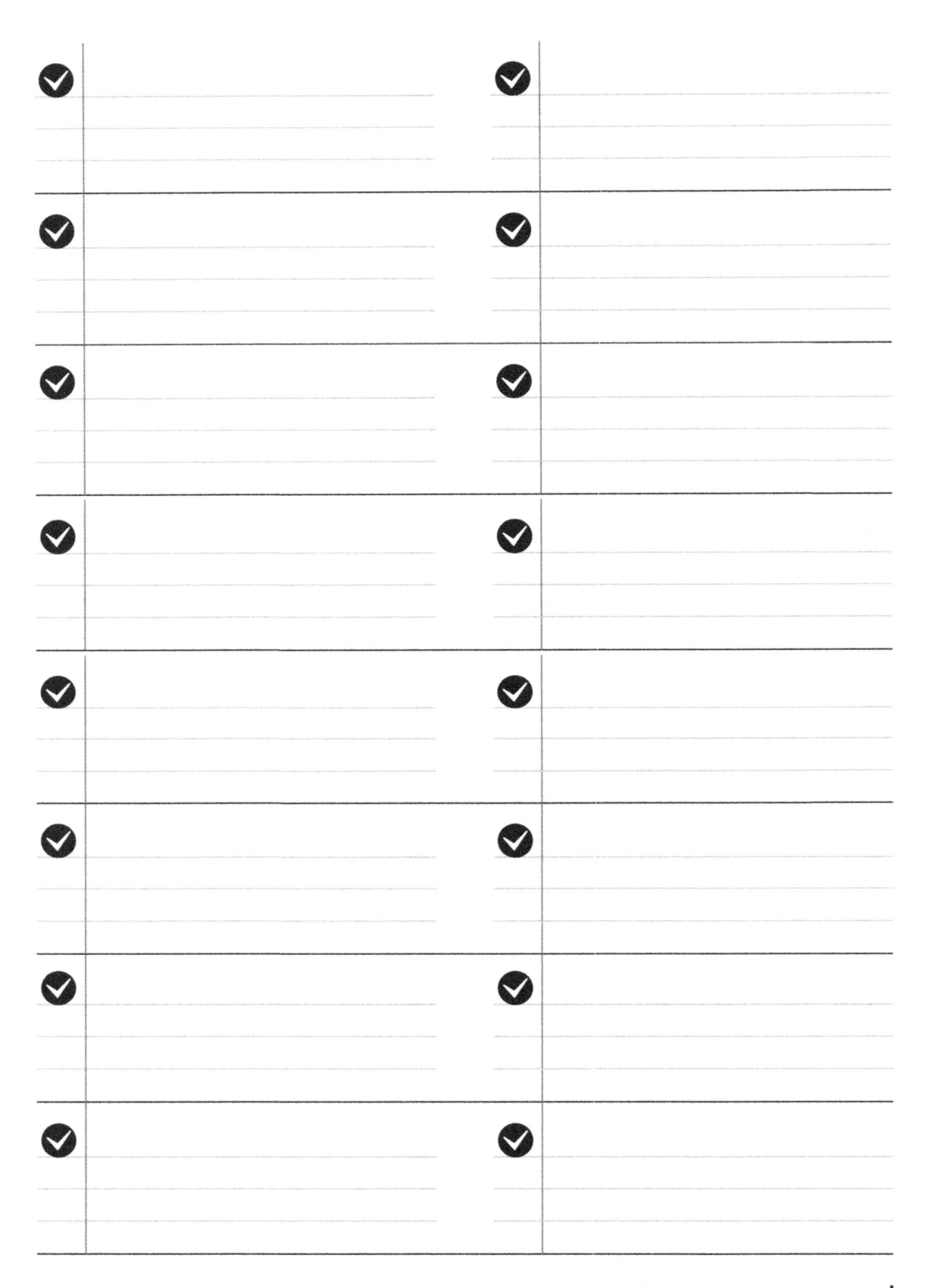

My Learning Journey

Congradulations!
112 words learned

My Learning Journey

Congradulations!
128 words learned

My Learning Journey

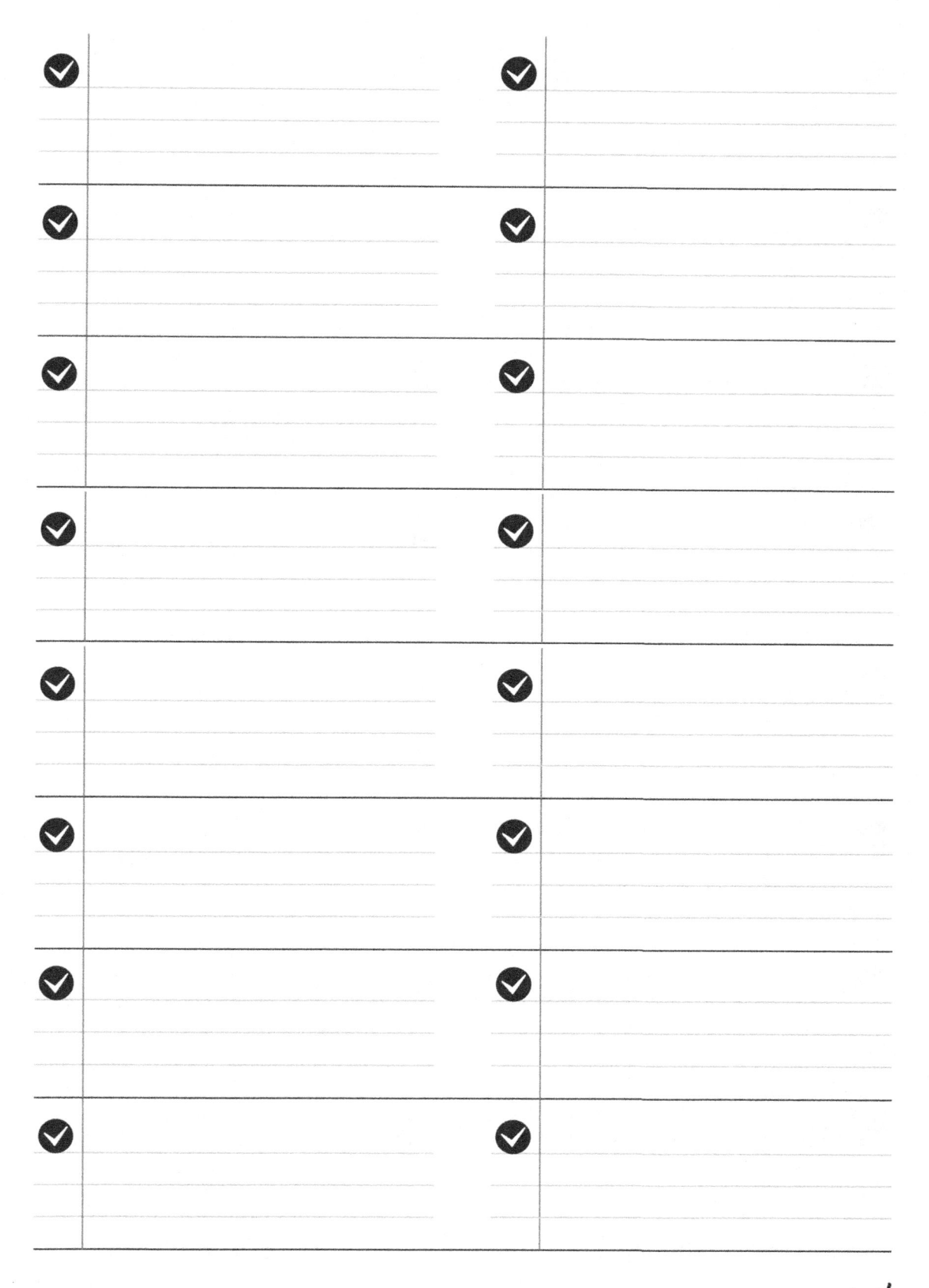

Congradulations!
144 words learned

My Learning Journey

Congradulations!
160 words learned

My Learning Journey

Congradulations!
176 words learned

My Learning Journey

Congradulations!
192 words learned

My Learning Journey

Congradulations!
208 words learned

My Learning Journey

Congradulations!
229 words learned

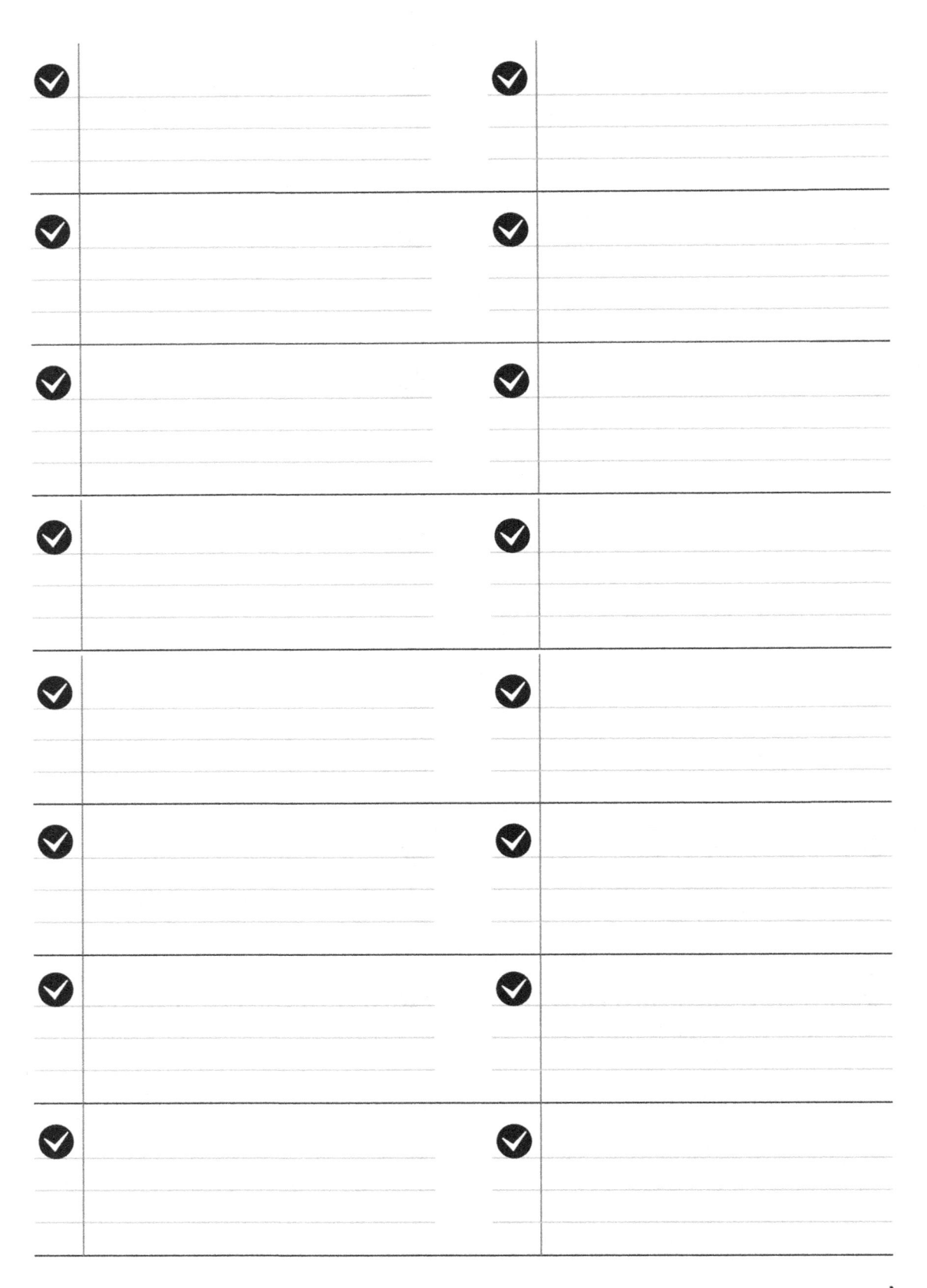

My Learning Journey

Congradulations!
240 words learned

My Learning Journey

Congradulations!
256 words learned

My Learning Journey

Congradulations!
272 words learned

My Learning Journey

Congradulations!
288 words learned

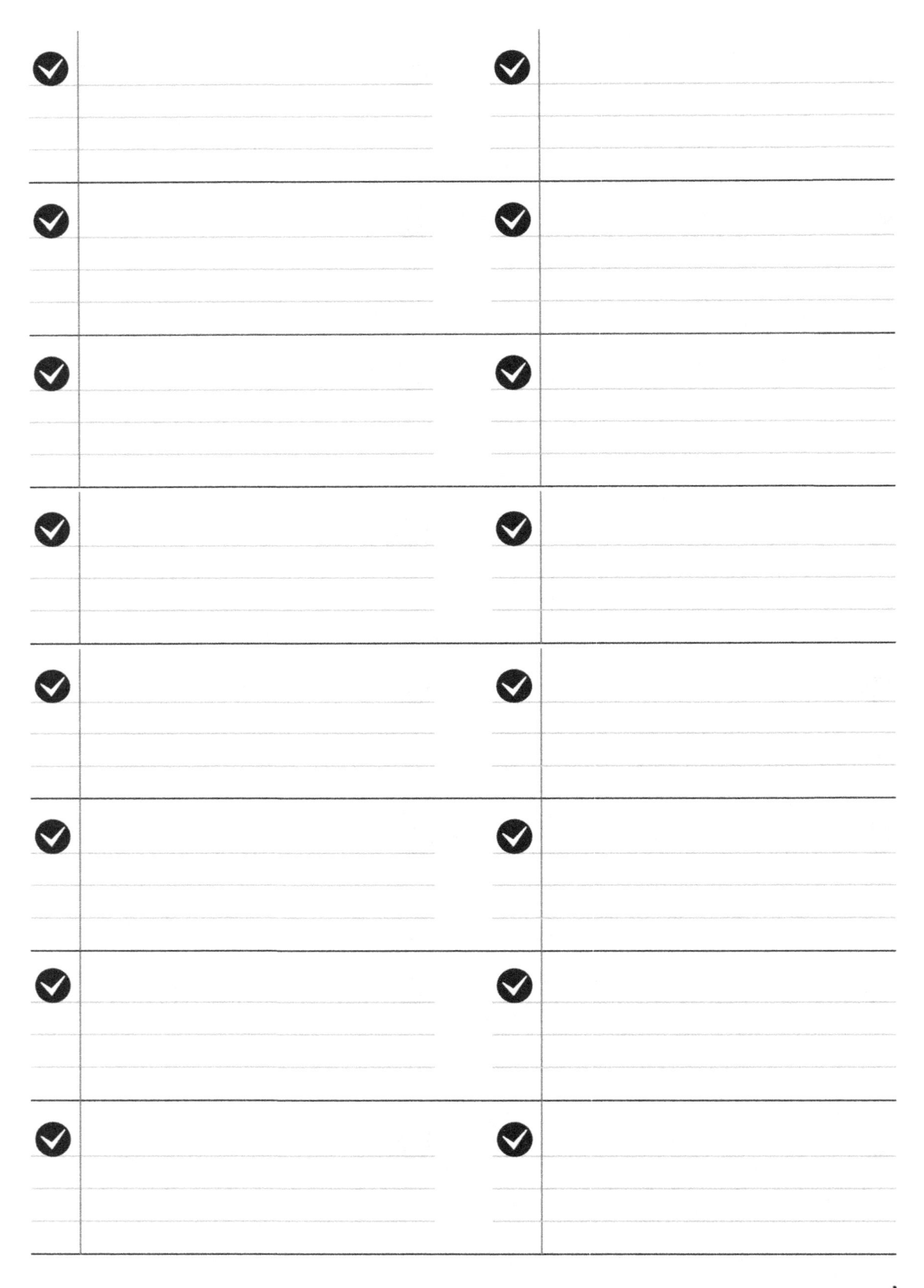

My Learning Journey

Congradulations!
304 words learned

My Learning Journey

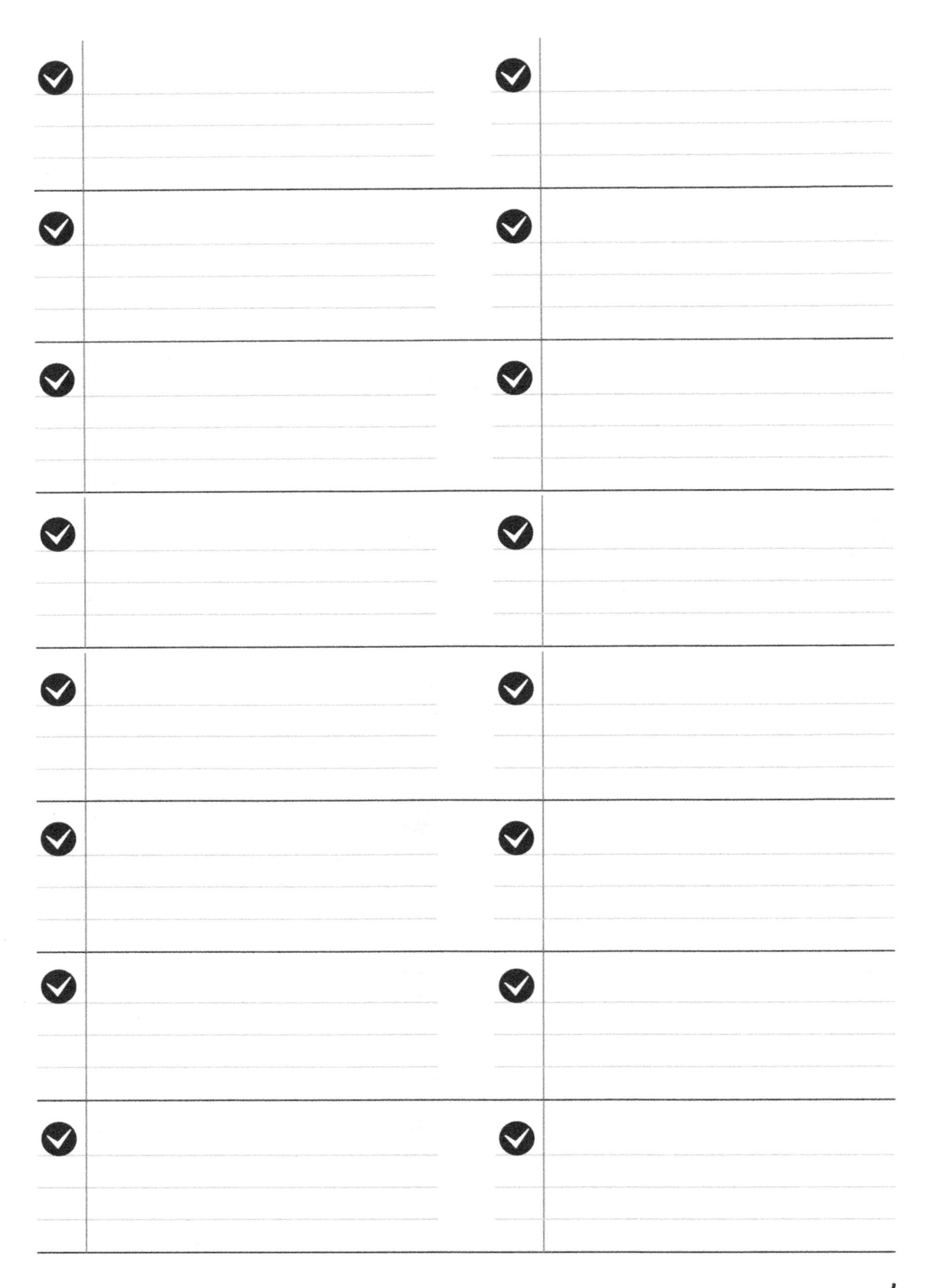

Congradulations!
320 words learned

My Learning Journey

Congradulations!
336 words learned

My Learning Journey

Congradulations!
352 words learned

My Learning Journey

Congratulations!
368 words learned

My Learning Journey

Congradulations!
384 words learned

My Learning Journey

Congradulations!
400 words learned

My Learning Journey

Congradulations!
916 words learned

My Learning Journey

Congradulations!
432 words learned

My Learning Journey

Congradulations!
998 words learned

My Learning Journey

Congradulations!
464 words learned

My Learning Journey

Congradulations!
480 words learned

My Learning Journey

Congradulations!
496 words learned

My Learning Journey

Congradulations!
512 words learned

My Learning Journey

Congradulations!
528 words learned

My Learning Journey

Congradulations!
544 words learned

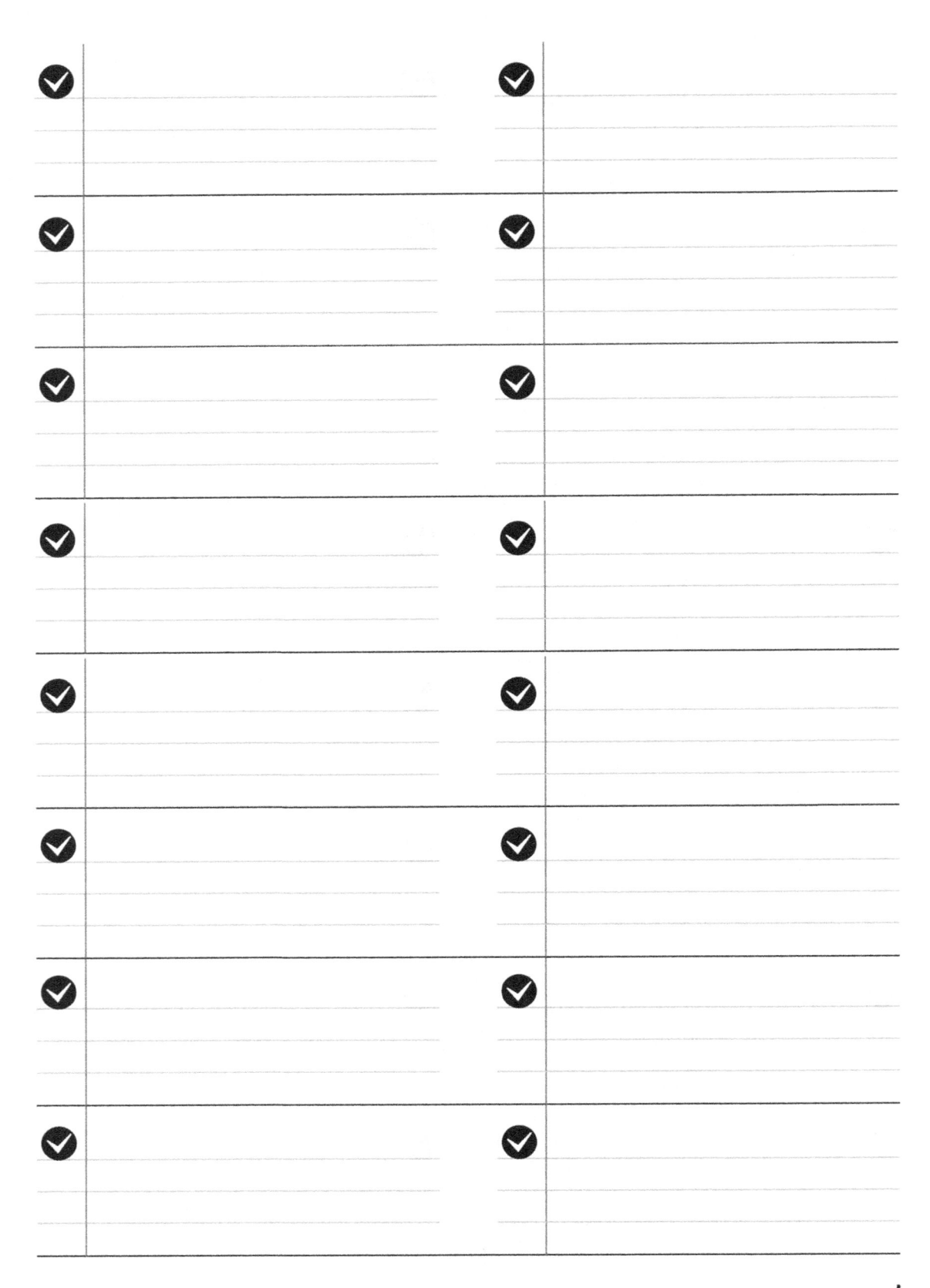

My Learning Journey

Congradulations!
560 words learned

560 Words

You got this!

LEAVE A WRITING SAMPLE ON THE NEXT PAGE. BE SURE TO COME BACK TO SEE HOW MUCH YOU'VE IMPROVED.

Writing Sample

My Learning Journey

Congradulations!
576 words learned

My Learning Journey

Congradulations!
592 words learned

My Learning Journey

Congradulations!
608 words learned

My Learning Journey

Congradulations!
629 words learned

My Learning Journey

Congradulations!
690 words learned

My Learning Journey

Congradulations!
656 words learned

My Learning Journey

Congradulations!
672 words learned

My Learning Journey

Congratulations!
688 words learned

My Learning Journey

Congradulations!
704 words learned

My Learning Journey

Congradulations!
720 words learned

My Learning Journey

Congradulations!
736 words learned

My Learning Journey

Congradulations!
752 words learned

My Learning Journey

Congradulations!
768 words learned

My Learning Journey

Congradulations!
784 words learned

My Learning Journey

Congradulations!
800 words learned

My Learning Journey

Congradulations!
816 words learned

My Learning Journey

Congradulations!
832 words learned

My Learning Journey

Congradulations!
898 words learned

My Learning Journey

Congradulations!
864 words learned

My Learning Journey

Congradulations!
880 words learned

My Learning Journey

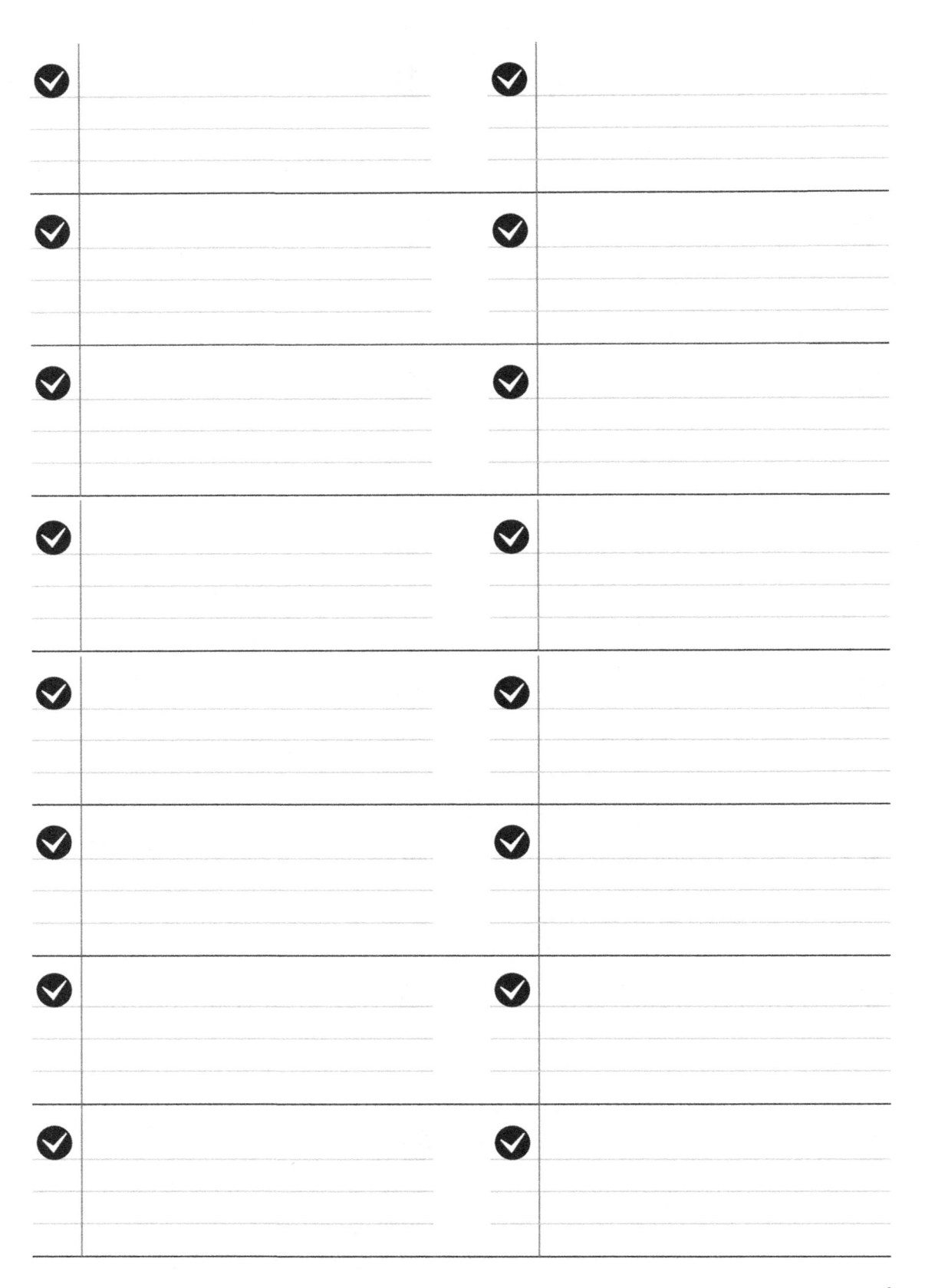

Congradulations!
896 words learned

My Learning Journey

Congradulations!
912 words learned

My Learning Journey

Congradulations!
928 words learned

My Learning Journey

Congradulations!
999 words learned

My Learning Journey

Congradulations!
960 words learned

My Learning Journey

Congradulations!
976 words learned

My Learning Journey

- ✓
- ✓
- ✓
- ✓
- ✓
- ✓
- ✓
- ✓
- ✓
- ✓
- ✓
- ✓
- ✓
- ✓
- ✓
- ✓

Congradulations!
992 words learned

My Learning Journey

Congradulations!
1008 words learned

My Learning Journey

Congradulations!
1024 words learned

My Learning Journey

Congradulations!
1040 words learned

My Learning Journey

Congradulations!
1056 words learned

My Learning Journey

Congradulations!
1072 words learned

My Learning Journey

Congradulations!
1088 words learned

My Learning Journey

Congradulations!
1104 words learned

My Learning Journey

Congradulations!
1120 words learned

My Learning Journey

Congradulations!
1136 words learned

My Learning Journey

Congradulations!
1152 words learned

My Learning Journey

Congradulations!
1168 words learned

My Learning Journey

Congradulations!
1184 words learned

My Learning Journey

**Congradulations!
1200 words learned**

My Learning Journey

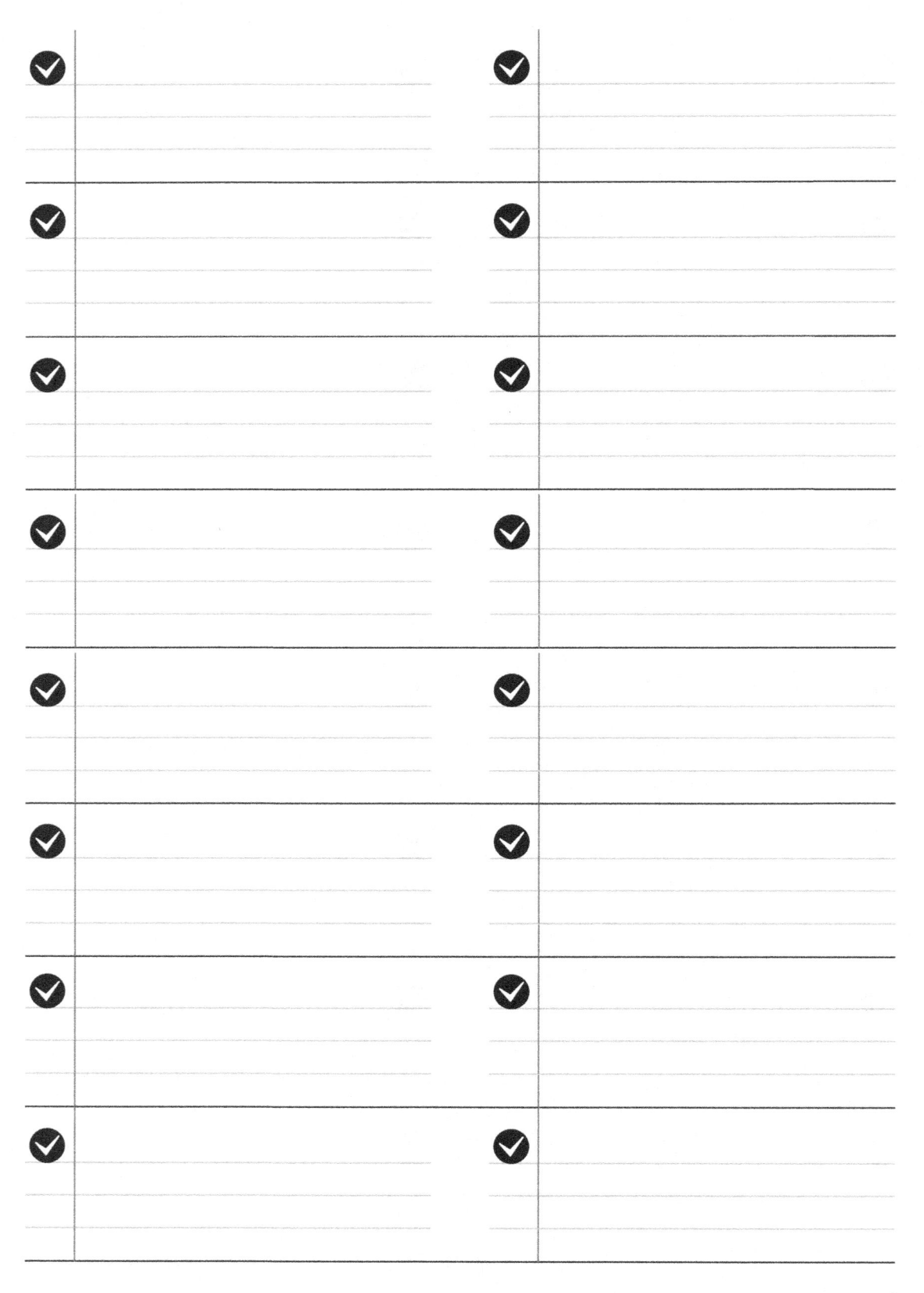

Congradulations!
1216 words learned

My Learning Journey

Congradulations!
1232 words learned

My Learning Journey

Congradulations!
1298 words learned

My Learning Journey

Congradulations!
1264 words learned

My Learning Journey

Congradulations!
1280 words learned

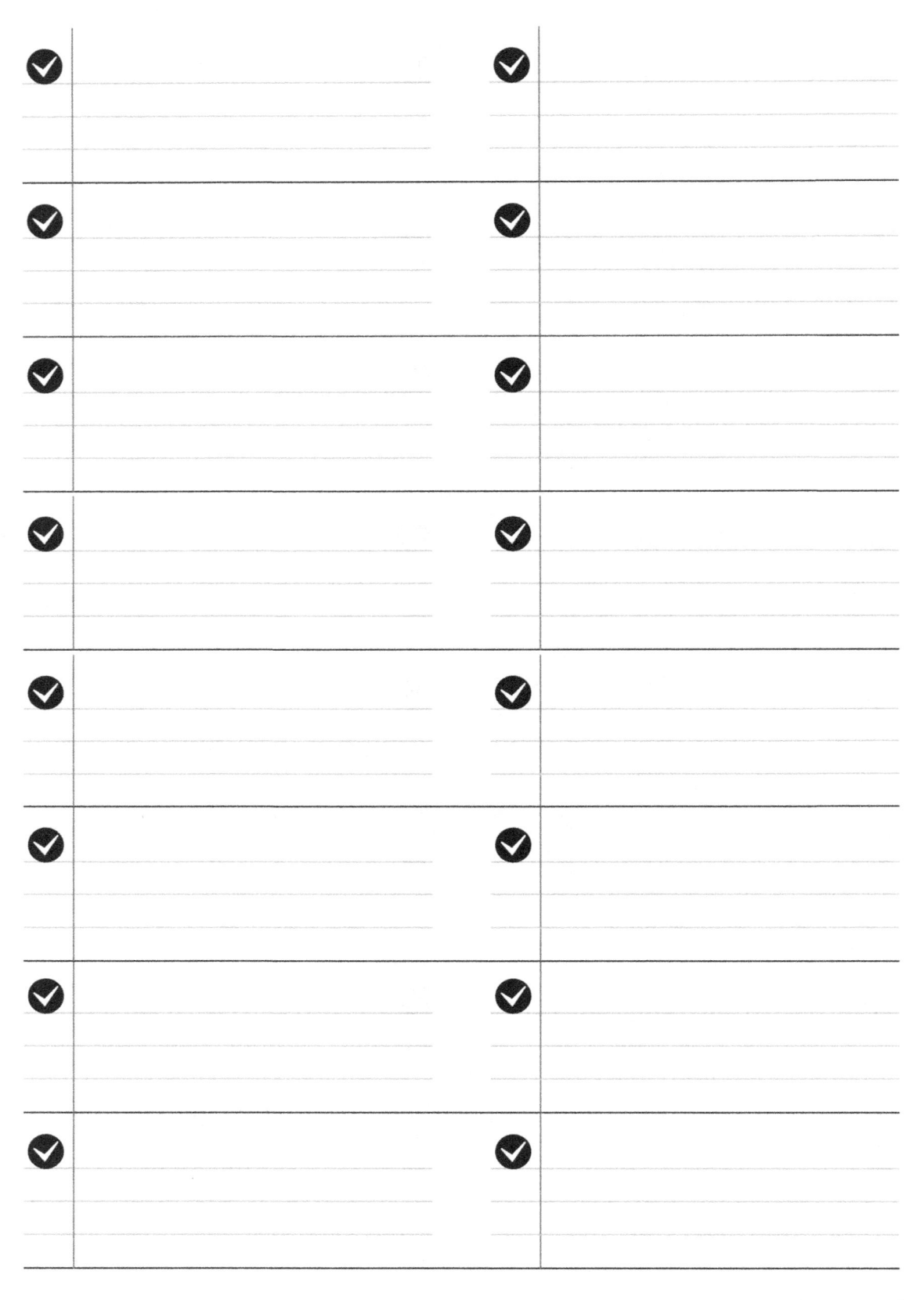

My Learning Journey

Congradulations!
1296 words learned

My Learning Journey

Congradulations!
1312 words learned

My Learning Journey

Congradulations!
1328 words learned

My Learning Journey

Congradulations!
1394 words learned

My Learning Journey

Congradulations!
1360 words learned

My Learning Journey

Congradulations!
1376 words learned

My Learning Journey

Congradulations!
1392 words learned

My Learning Journey

Congradulations!
1908 words learned

My Learning Journey

Congradulations!
1924 words learned

My Learning Journey

Congradulations!
1990 words learned

My Learning Journey

Congradulations!
1956 words learned

My Learning Journey

Congradulations!
1972 words learned

My Learning Journey

Congradulations!
1988 words learned

My Learning Journey

Congradulations!
1509 words learned

1504 Words

You're making this look easy!

LEAVE A WRITING SAMPLE ON THE NEXT PAGE. BE SURE TO COME BACK TO SEE HOW MUCH YOU'VE IMPROVED.

Writing Sample

My Learning Journey

Congradulations!
1520 words learned

My Learning Journey

Congradulations!
1536 words learned

My Learning Journey

Congradulations!
1552 words learned

My Learning Journey

Congradulations!
1568 words learned

My Learning Journey

Congradulations!
1584 words learned

My Learning Journey

Congradulations!
1600 words learned

My Learning Journey

Congradulations!
1616 words learned

My Learning Journey

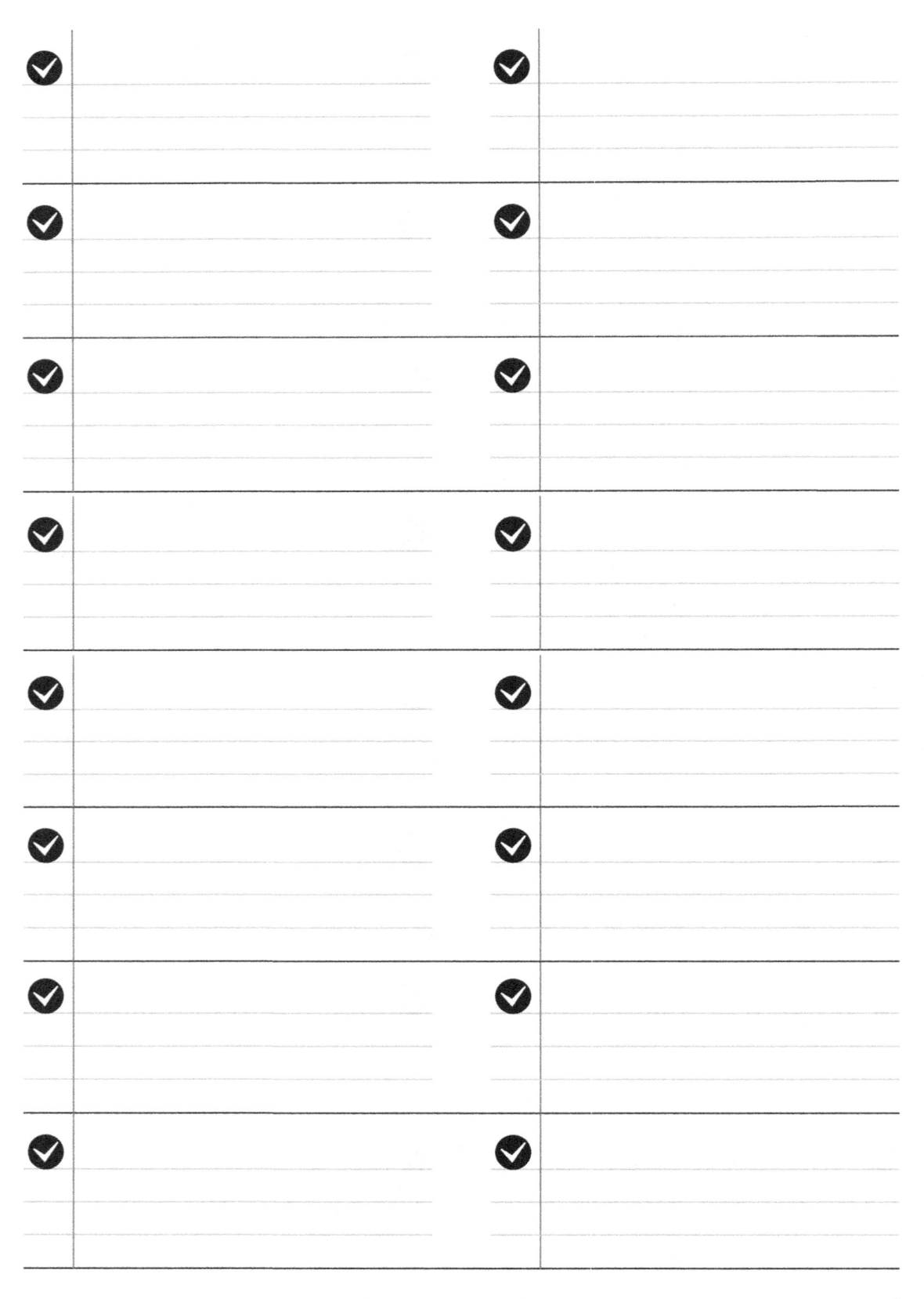

Congradulations!
1632 words learned

My Learning Journey

Congradulations!
1648 words learned

My Learning Journey

Congradulations!
1664 words learned

My Learning Journey

Congradulations!
1680 words learned

My Learning Journey

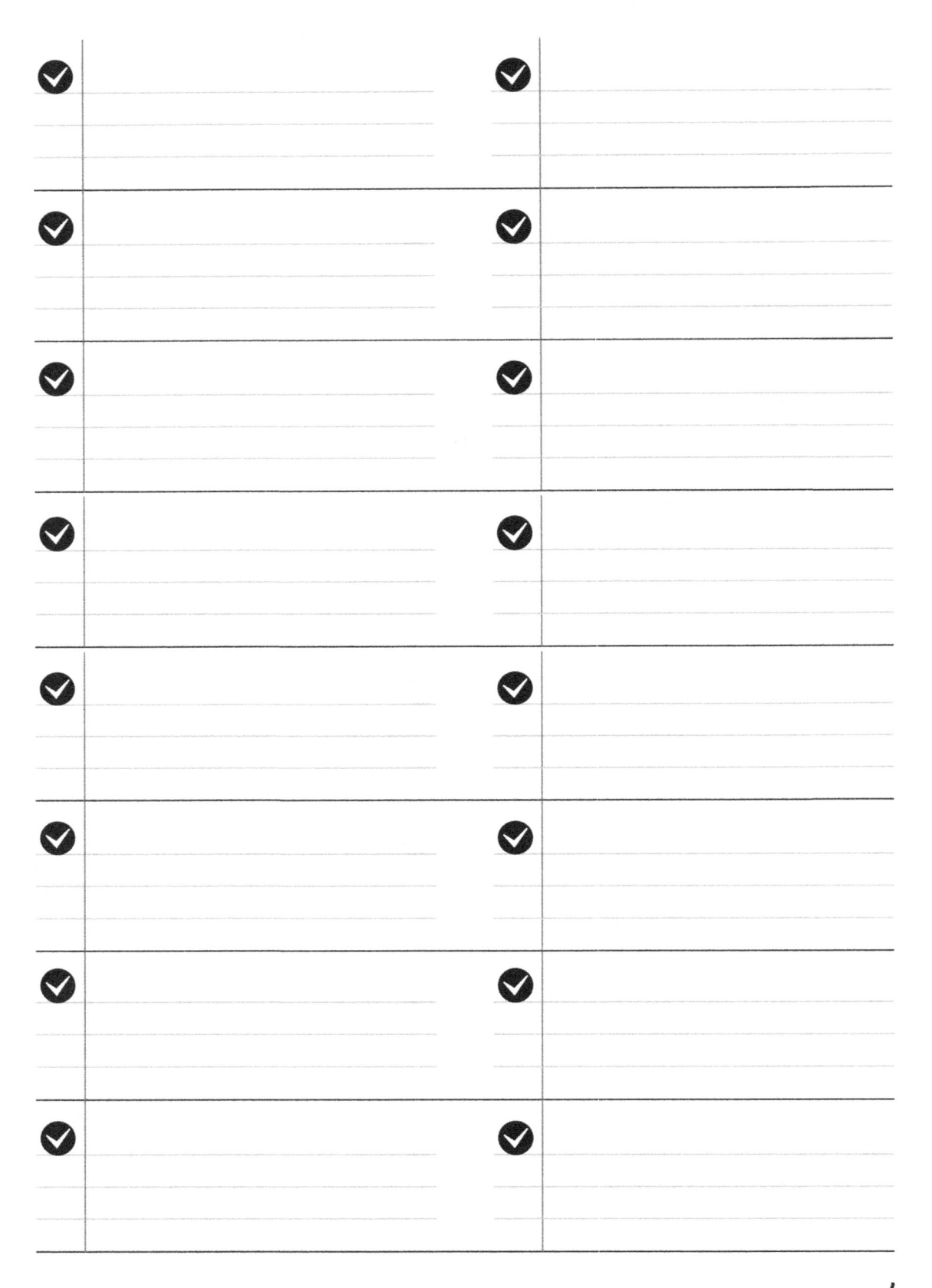

Congradulations!
1696 words learned

My Learning Journey

Congradulations!
1712 words learned

My Learning Journey

Congradulations!
1728 words learned

My Learning Journey

Congradulations!
1799 words learned

My Learning Journey

Congradulations!
1760 words learned

My Learning Journey

Congradulations!
1776 words learned

My Learning Journey

Congradulations!
1792 words learned

My Learning Journey

Congradulations!
1808 words learned

My Learning Journey

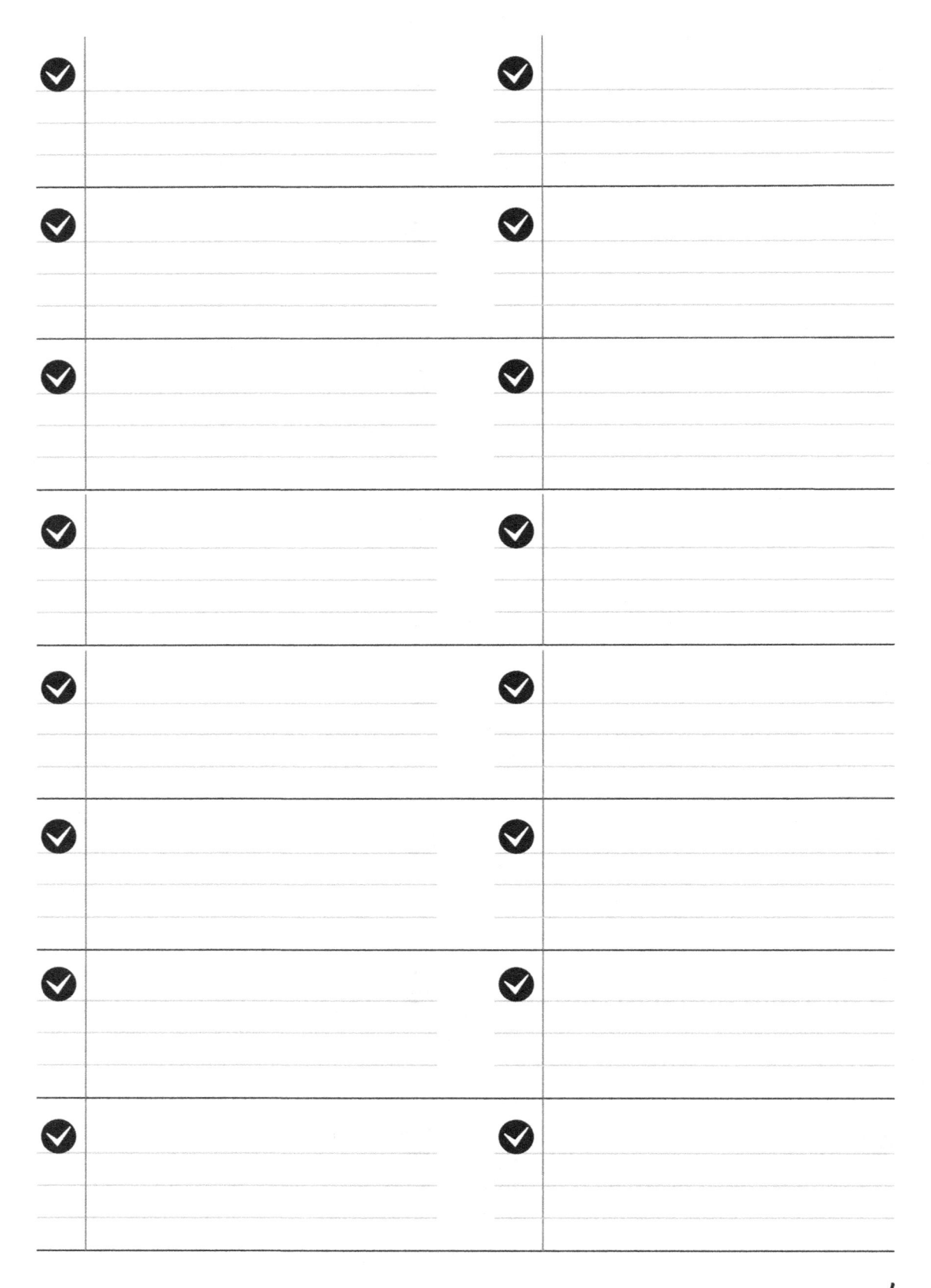

Congradulations!
1824 words learned

My Learning Journey

Congradulations!
1840 words learned

My Learning Journey

Congradulations!
1856 words learned

My Learning Journey

Congradulations!
1872 words learned

My Learning Journey

Congradulations!
1888 words learned

My Learning Journey

Congradulations!
1904 words learned

My Learning Journey

Congradulations!
1920 words learned

My Learning Journey

Congradulations!
1936 words learned

My Learning Journey

Congradulations!
1952 words learned

My Learning Journey

Congradulations!
1968 words learned

My Learning Journey

Congradulations!
1984 words learned

My Learning Journey

Congradulations!
2000 words learned

My Learning Journey

Congradulations!
2016 words learned

My Learning Journey

Congradulations!

2032 words learned

My Learning Journey

Congradulations!
2098 words learned

My Learning Journey

Congradulations!

2064 words learned

My Learning Journey

Congradulations!
2080 words learned

My Learning Journey

Congradulations!
2096 words learned

My Learning Journey

Congradulations!
2112 words learned

My Learning Journey

Congradulations!
2128 words learned

My Learning Journey

Congradulations!
2194 words learned

My Learning Journey

Congradulations!
2160 words learned

My Learning Journey

Congradulations!
2176 words learned

My Learning Journey

Congradulations!
2192 words learned

My Learning Journey

Congradulations!
2208 words learned

My Learning Journey

Congradulations!

2224 words learned

My Learning Journey

Congradulations!
2290 words learned

My Learning Journey

Congradulations!
2256 words learned

My Learning Journey

Congradulations!
2272 words learned

My Learning Journey

Congradulations!
2288 words learned

My Learning Journey

Congradulations!
2304 words learned

My Learning Journey

Congradulations!
2320 words learned

My Learning Journey

Congradulations!

2336 words learned

My Learning Journey

Congradulations!
2352 words learned

My Learning Journey

Congradulations!
2368 words learned

My Learning Journey

Congradulations!

2384 words learned

My Learning Journey

Congradulations!
2400 words learned

My Learning Journey

Congradulations!
2416 words learned

My Learning Journey

Congradulations!

2432 words learned

My Learning Journey

Congradulations!
2448 words learned

My Learning Journey

Congradulations!
2464 words learned

My Learning Journey

Congradulations!
2,480 words learned

My Learning Journey

Congradulations!
2496 words learned

My Learning Journey

Congradulations!
2512 words learned

My Learning Journey

Congradulations!
2528 words learned

My Learning Journey

Congradulations!
2544 words learned

My Learning Journey

Congradulations!
2560 words learned

My Learning Journey

Congradulations!
2576 words learned

My Learning Journey

Congradulations!
2592 words learned

My Learning Journey

Congradulations!
2608 words learned

My Learning Journey

Congratulations!
2624 words learned

My Learning Journey

Congradulations!
2640 words learned

My Learning Journey

Congradulations!
2,656 words learned

My Learning Journey

Congradulations!
2672 words learned

My Learning Journey

Congradulations!
2688 words learned

My Learning Journey

Congradulations!
2704 words learned

My Learning Journey

Congradulations!
2720 words learned

My Learning Journey

Congradulations!
2736 words learned

My Learning Journey

Congradulations!
2752 words learned

My Learning Journey

Congradulations!
2768 words learned

My Learning Journey

Congradulations!
2784 words learned

My Learning Journey

Congradulations!
2800 words learned

My Learning Journey

Congradulations!
2816 words learned

My Learning Journey

Congradulations!
2832 words learned

My Learning Journey

Congradulations!

2848 words learned

My Learning Journey

Congradulations!
2864 words learned

My Learning Journey

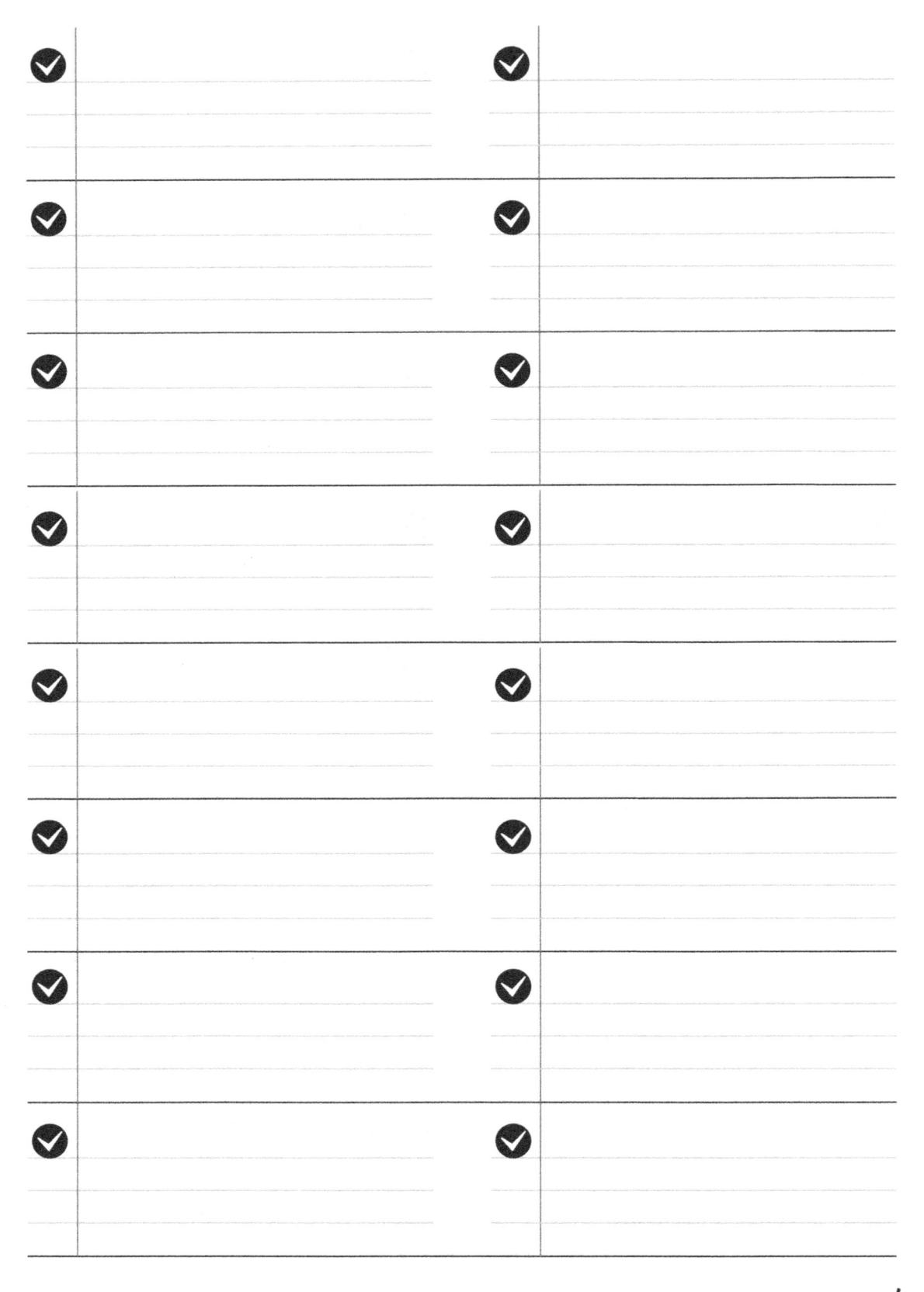

Congradulations!
2880 words learned

My Learning Journey

Congradulations!

2896 words learned

My Learning Journey

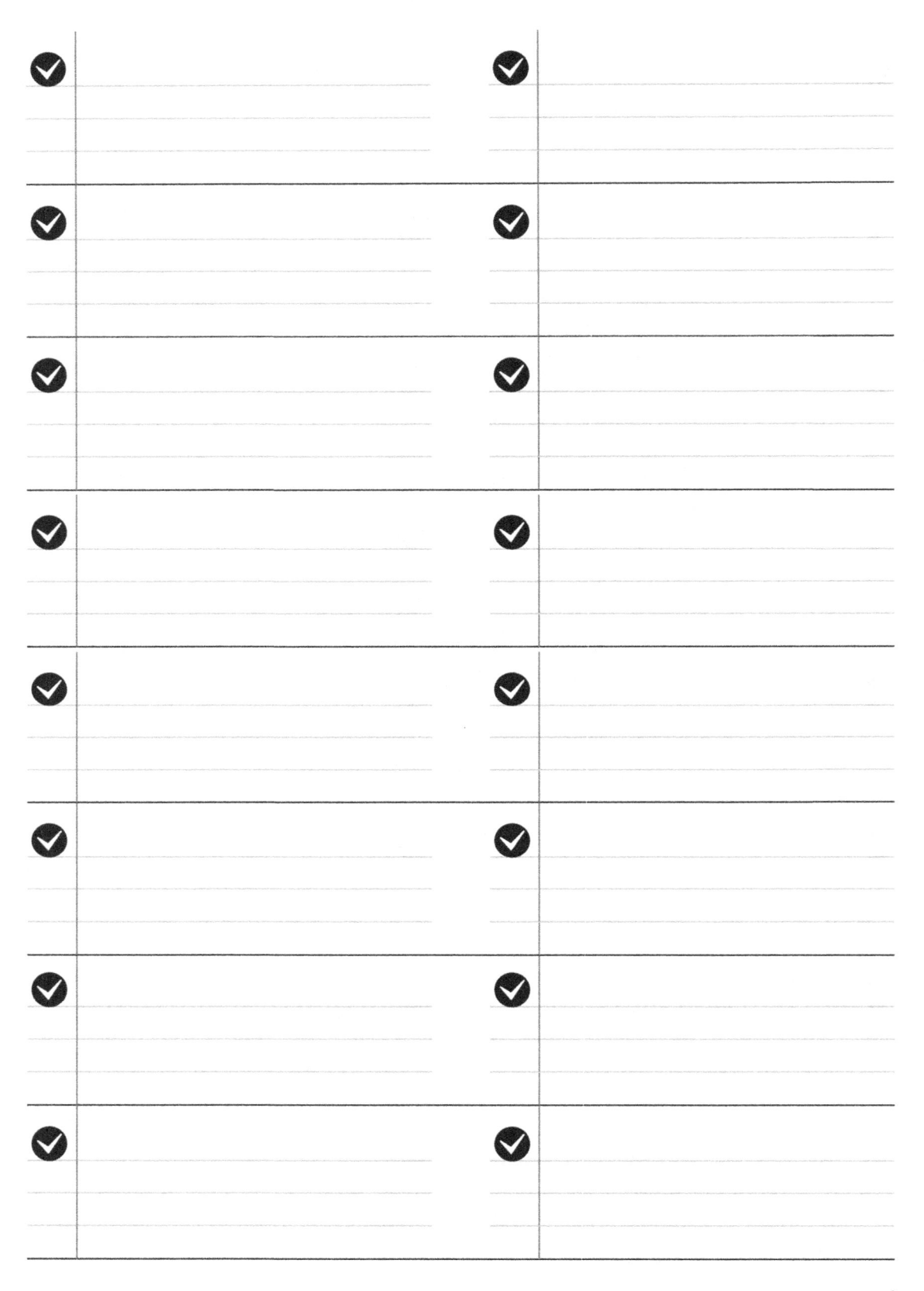

Congradulations!
2912 words learned

My Learning Journey

Congradulations!
2928 words learned

My Learning Journey

Congradulations!
2999 words learned

My Learning Journey

Congradulations!
2960 words learned

My Learning Journey

Congradulations!
2976 words learned

My Learning Journey

Congradulations!
2992 words learned

My Learning Journey

Congradulations!
3008 words learned

3008 Words

You're almost there!

LEAVE A WRITING SAMPLE ON THE NEXT PAGE. BE SURE TO COME BACK TO SEE HOW MUCH YOU'VE IMPROVED.

Writing Sample

My Learning Journey

Congradulations!
3024 words learned

My Learning Journey

Congradulations!
3090 words learned

My Learning Journey

Congradulations!
3056 words learned

My Learning Journey

Congratulations!
3072 words learned

My Learning Journey

Congradulations!
3088 words learned

My Learning Journey

Congradulations!
3104 words learned

My Learning Journey

Congradulations!
3120 words learned

My Learning Journey

Congradulations!
3136 words learned

My Learning Journey

Congradulations!
3152 words learned

My Learning Journey

Congradulations!
3168 words learned

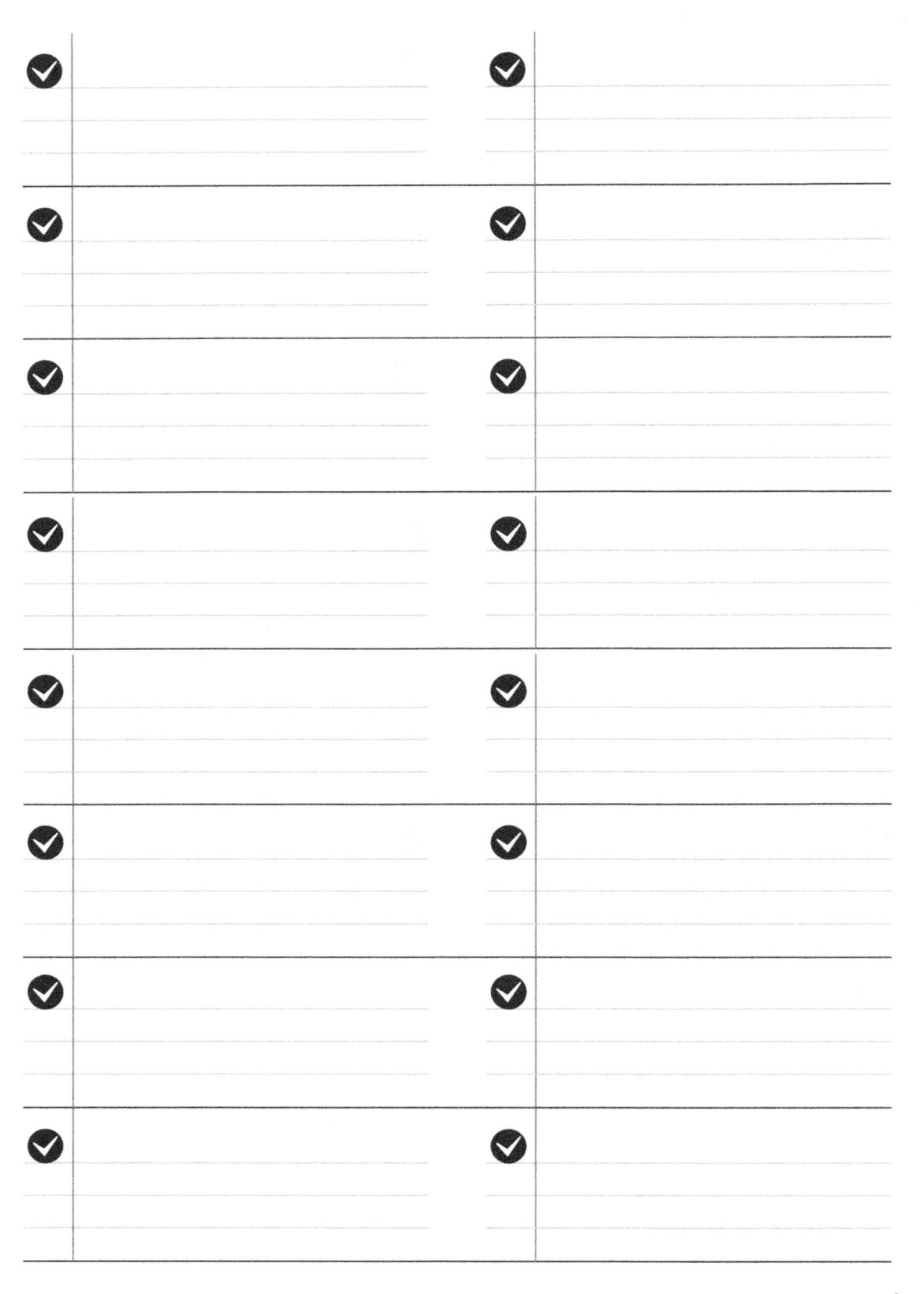

My Learning Journey

Congradulations!
3184 words learned

My Learning Journey

Congradulations!
3200 words learned

My Learning Journey

Congradulations!
3216 words learned

My Learning Journey

Congradulations!
3232 words learned

My Learning Journey

Congradulations!
3298 words learned

My Learning Journey

Congradulations!
3264 words learned

My Learning Journey

Congradulations!
3280 words learned

My Learning Journey

Congradulations!
3296 words learned

My Learning Journey

Congradulations!
3312 words learned

My Learning Journey

Congradulations!
3328 words learned

My Learning Journey

Congradulations!
3344 words learned

My Learning Journey

Congradulations!
3360 words learned

My Learning Journey

Congradulations!
3376 words learned

My Learning Journey

Congradulations!
3392 words learned

My Learning Journey

Congradulations!
3408 words learned

My Learning Journey

Congradulations!
3424 words learned

My Learning Journey

Congradulations!
3440 words learned

My Learning Journey

Congradulations!
3456 words learned

My Learning Journey

Congradulations!
3972 words learned

My Learning Journey

Congradulations!
3988 words learned

My Learning Journey

Congradulations!
3504 words learned

My Learning Journey

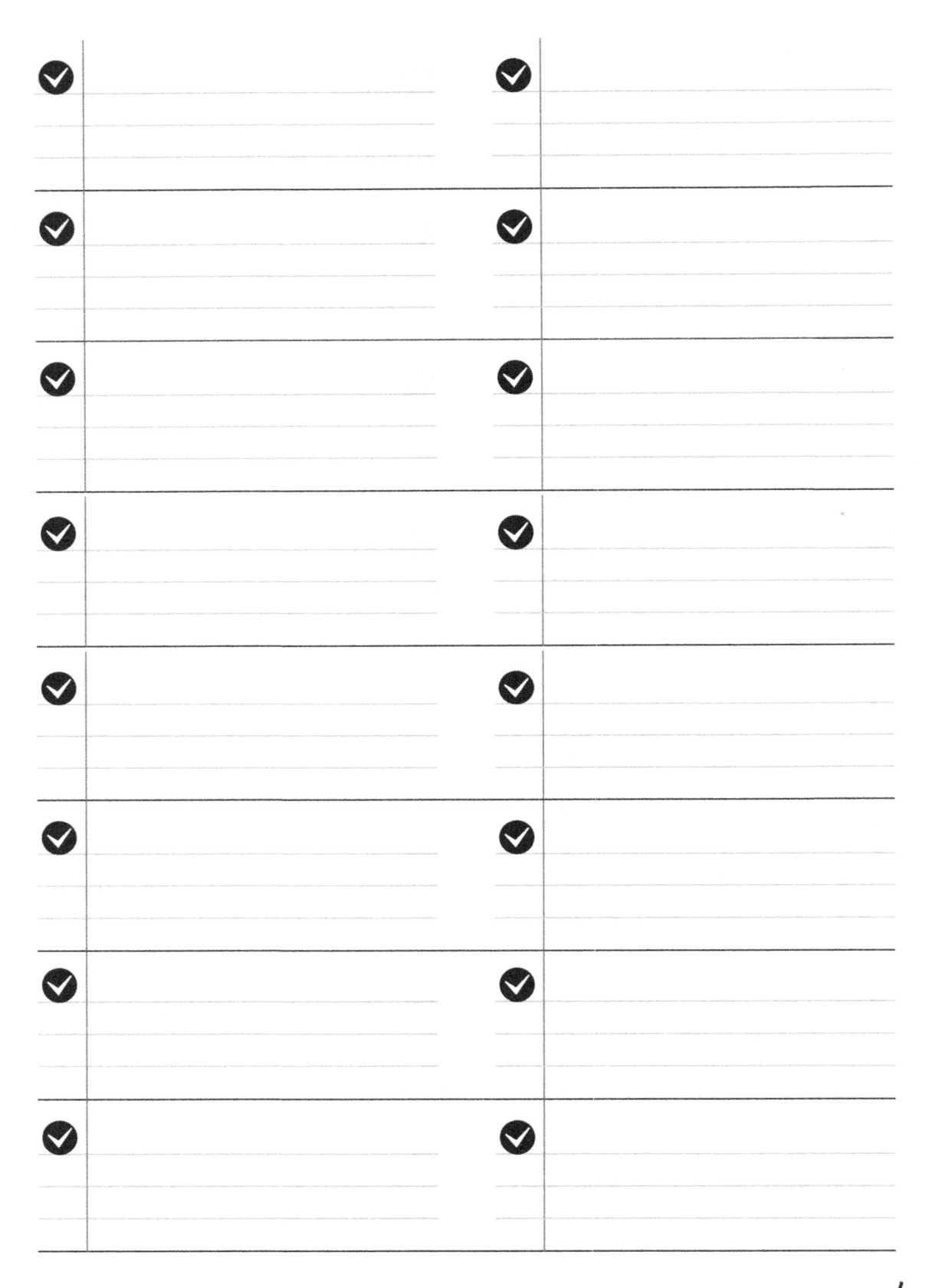

Congradulations!
3520 words learned

My Learning Journey

Congradulations!
3536 words learned

My Learning Journey

Congradulations!
3552 words learned

My Learning Journey

Congradulations!
3568 words learned

My Learning Journey

Congradulations!
3584 words learned

My Learning Journey

Congradulations!
3600 words learned

My Learning Journey

Congradulations!
3616 words learned

My Learning Journey

Congradulations!
3632 words learned

My Learning Journey

Congradulations!
3648 words learned

My Learning Journey

Congradulations!
3664 words learned

My Learning Journey

Congradulations!
3680 words learned

My Learning Journey

Congradulations!
3696 words learned

My Learning Journey

Congradulations!
3712 words learned

My Learning Journey

Congradulations!
3728 words learned

My Learning Journey

Congradulations!
3799 words learned

My Learning Journey

Congradulations!
3760 words learned

My Learning Journey

Congradulations!
3776 words learned

My Learning Journey

Congradulations!
3792 words learned

My Learning Journey

Congradulations!
3808 words learned

My Learning Journey

Congradulations!
3824 words learned

My Learning Journey

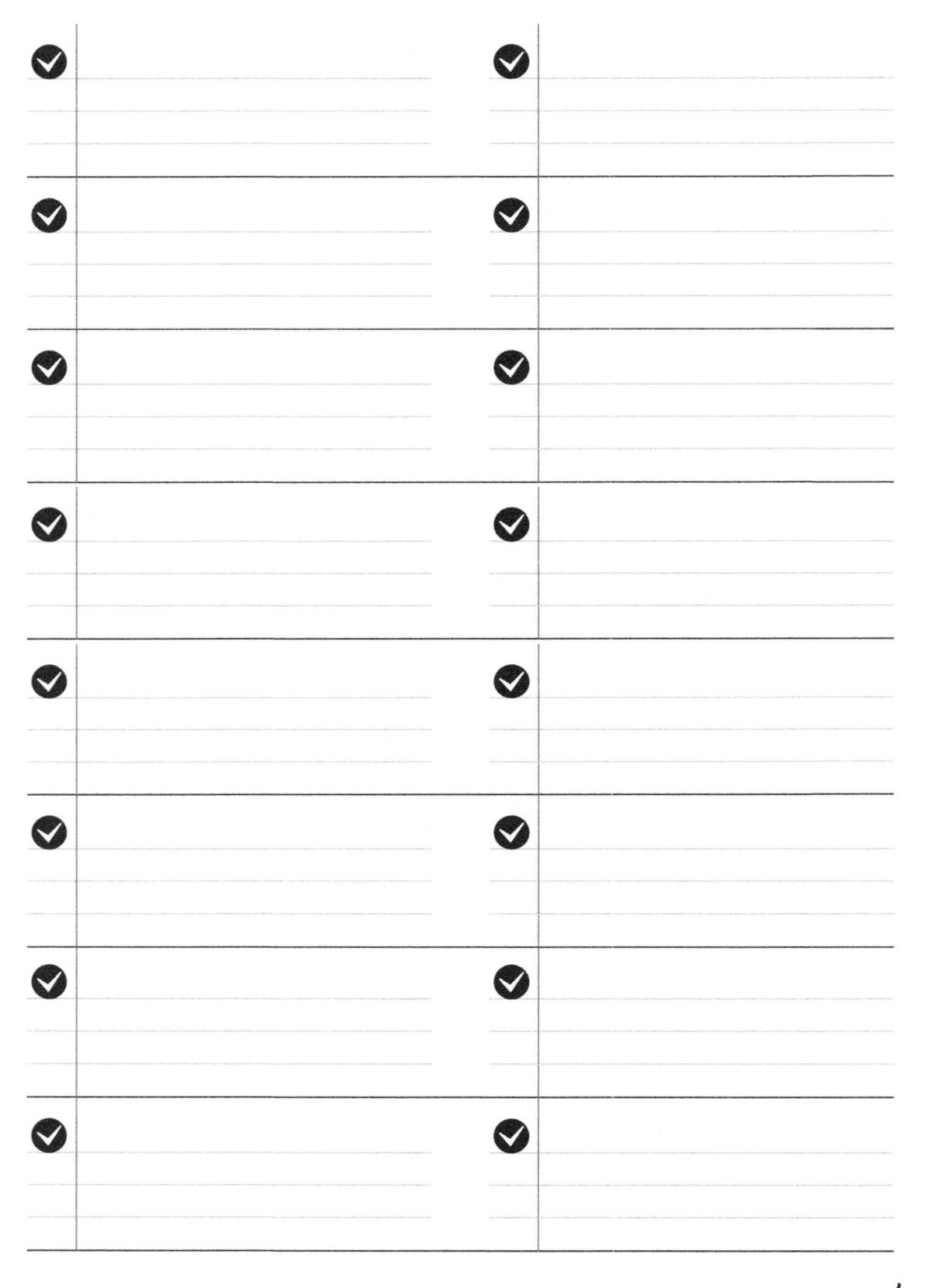

Congradulations!
3890 words learned

My Learning Journey

Congratulations!
3856 words learned

My Learning Journey

Congradulations!
3872 words learned

My Learning Journey

Congradulations!
3888 words learned

My Learning Journey

Congradulations!
3904 words learned

My Learning Journey

Congradulations!
3920 words learned

My Learning Journey

Congradulations!
3936 words learned

My Learning Journey

Congradulations!
3952 words learned

My Learning Journey

Congradulations!
3968 words learned

My Learning Journey

Congradulations!
3984 words learned

My Learning Journey

Congradulations!
4000 words learned

4000 Words Learned

You made it to the end of this workbook!

REMEMBER, THIS IS JUST THE BEGINNING OF YOUR LANGUAGE-LEARNING JOURNEY. STEP OUT, EMBRACE OPPORTUNITIES, AND USE YOUR NEWLY ACQUIRED LANGUAGE AS FREQUENTLY AS POSSIBLE. EACH USE WILL NOT ONLY ENHANCE YOUR CONFIDENCE BUT ALSO SHARPEN YOUR COMMUNICATION SKILLS, MAKING YOU FEEL MORE EMPOWERED IN YOUR LANGUAGE JOURNEY.

ON THE NEXT PAGE, LEAVE YOUR FINAL WRITING SAMPLE, AND THEN GO BACK TO YOUR FIRST WRITING SAMPLE TO SEE HOW MUCH YOU'VE IMPROVED.

Writing Sample

Made in United States
Orlando, FL
23 July 2024